SIMPLE BIKE MAINTENANCE

Time for a Tune-Up!

BY LISA J. AMSTUTZ

Gail Saunders-Smith, PhD,
consulting editor

Pebble Plus is published by Capstone Press,
1710 Roe Crest Drive, North Mankato, Minnesota 56003.
www.capstonepub.com

Library of Congress Cataloging-in-Publication Data
Amstutz, Lisa J.
Simple bike maintenance : time for a tune-up / by Lisa J. Amstutz.
pages cm.—(Pebble Plus. Spokes)
Includes bibliographical references and index.
Summary: "Full-color photos and simple text provide an overview of basic bicycle maintenance"—Provided by publisher.
ISBN 978-1-4765-3966-9 (library binding)
ISBN 978-1-4765-6029-8 (ebook pdf)
1. Bicycles—Maintenance and repair. I.Title.
TL430.A5 2014
629.28'772—dc23   2013031429

Editorial Credits
Jeni Wittrock, editor; Kyle Grenz, designer; Jennifer Walker, production specialist; Sarah Shuette, photo stylist;
Marcy Morin, photo scheduler

Photo Credits
Alamy: Alvey & Towers Picture Library, 13; BananaStock, Ltd., 17; Capstone Studio: Karon Dubke, 9, 15, 19; Getty Images: The Image Bank/Ariel Skelley, 5; iStockphotos: BartCo, 21, Ed Hidden, 7, ktmoffitt, 11; Shutterstock: Sergiy Zavgorodny, cover

Design Elements:
Shutterstock: filip robert, Kalmatsuy Tatyana

Note to Parents and Teachers

The Spokes set supports national science standards related to safety and recreation. This book describes and illustrates simple bicycle maintenance and upkeep. The images support early readers in understanding the text. The repetition of words and phrases helps early readers learn new words. This book also introduces early readers to subject-specific vocabulary words, which are defined in the Glossary section. Early readers may need assistance to read some words and to use the Table of Contents, Glossary, Read More, Internet Sites, and Index sections of the book.

Printed in the United States of America in North Mankato, Minnesota.
092013   007775CGS14.

Table of Contents

Bikes Need Care

A bike takes you where
you need to go. But a rusty
or broken bike is hard to use.
Take care of your bike so
you're always ready to ride.

Before You Ride

Full tires keep your bike rolling.

Tires should feel firm. If not,

an adult can help you add air.

Use a tire pump to fill the tires.

Look carefully at the
grooves in the tires.
Remove any chunks of dirt
or rocks from the tread.
Check for cuts or holes.

tire treads

Safety Check

Loose bike parts are unsafe.

Hold the front wheel steady.

Try to turn the handlebars.

If they wiggle, tighten them.

The seat should be tight too.

Does your bike have hand
brakes? Roll the bike forward
and squeeze one brake.
The bike should stop quickly.
Now test the other brake.

hand brake

After You Ride

Clean a dirty bike with water and soap. Rinse and dry it well. Park your bike indoors or cover it. Wet bikes rust!

After washing your bike,

lube the chain to prevent rust.

Add chain oil as you turn

the pedals backward.

Wipe off drips with a rag.

Tune-up Time

Once or twice a year, give

the bike a full wash and wax.

Degrease the chain and wipe

it clean. Then lube it again.

Once a year take your bike
to a bike shop. Let a pro
give your bike a full checkup.
A little extra care will keep
you pedaling safely!

Glossary

chain oil—a type of oil used on bike chains; chain oil keeps bike gears and chains running smoothly

degrease—to remove grease or oil using a special cleaner

lube—to apply oil or grease

maintain—to keep in good shape

rust—to become covered in a reddish brown substance; rust forms when iron or steel stays wet

tire pump—a tool used for adding air to a tire

tread—a series of bumps and grooves on a tire

wax—to put wax or polish on something; wax keeps bikes from rusting

Read More

Mara, Wil. *What Should I Do? On My Bike.* Community Connections. Ann Arbor, Mich.: Cherry Lake Pub., 2012.

Hamilton, Robert M. *On a Bike.* Going Places. New York: Gareth Stevens Pub., 2012.

Herrington, Lisa M. *Bicycle Safety.* Rookie Read-About Safety. New York: Children's Press, 2012.

Internet Sites

FactHound offers a safe, fun way to find Internet sites related to this book. All of the sites on FactHound have been researched by our staff.

Here's all you do:

Visit *www.facthound.com*

Type in this code: 9781476539669

Check out projects, games and lots more at
www.capstonekids.com

Index

Word Count: 230
Grade: 1
Early-Intervention Level: 15